The Master Of Vying Exam

K. Ahram

Published by K. Ahram, 2024.

THE MASTER OF VYING EXAM

First edition. April 20, 2024.

ISBN: 979-8223494959

Written by K. Ahram.

Table of Contents

.... 1

Book Introduction: 2

OVERVIEW 4

1: Understanding the Competitive Exam Landscape 7

2: Setting SMART Goals for Success 9

3: Crafting an Effective Study Plan 13

4: Mastering Time Management Techniques 16

5: Strategies for Effective Note-taking and Revision 20

6: Enhancing Memory and Retention Skills 24

7: Practicing with Mock Tests and Sample Papers 27

8: Analyzing and Learning from Mistakes 30

9 : Improving Speed and Accuracy in Problem Solving 33

10: CONSISTENCY 38

11: Staying Motivated Throughout the Preparation Journey 43

12: HOW TO USE AI 48

13: SETBACKS 51

14: ENCOURAGE YOURSELF 54

15: WHY STRESS 56

16: 0VERCOME STRESS 58

17: BAD GOVERNMENT 62

18: Balancing Studies with Personal Life and Responsibilities 65

19: SUCCESS STORIES 71

About Author

Hello! My pen name is K.Ahram and I am a beginner writer. Writing has been a passion of mine for as long as I can remember, but I have only recently mustered the courage to share my work with others. As a beginner, I understand that I have much to learn about the craft and I am excited to explore new genres, styles, and techniques. I am eager to connect with other writers, receive feedback on my work, and continue to improve my skills. Though I am just starting out on this writing journey, I am determined to learn and grow as a writer and share my stories with the world.

Writing is a way to explore the depths of my imagination, express my thoughts and emotions, and connect with others through the power of storytelling, I find immense joy in the process of putting pen to paper or fingers to keyboard.

Book Introduction:

Welcome to "Mastering Competitive Exams: A Comprehensive Guide." In this book, we embark on a journey to equip you with the knowledge, strategies, and mindset needed to excel in competitive exams. Whether you're preparing for college entrance exams, professional certifications, or any other competitive test, this guide is your roadmap to success.

Competitive exams are not just about testing your knowledge; they are about testing your preparation, strategy, and resilience. With the right approach, anyone can crack these exams and achieve their academic or professional goals. This book is designed to help you navigate through the challenges of competitive exam preparation, providing you with practical tips, expert advice, and actionable strategies at every step of the way.

Over the course of these chapters, you'll learn how to understand the competitive exam landscape, set achievable goals, create an effective study plan, manage your time efficiently, overcome exam anxiety, and much more. Each chapter is packed with detailed information, real-life examples, and exercises to reinforce your learning.

Whether you're a seasoned exam-taker looking to improve your scores or a beginner just starting your preparation journey, this book has something for everyone. So, let's dive in and begin your transformation from an aspiring candidate to a confident exam conqueror!

OVERVIEW

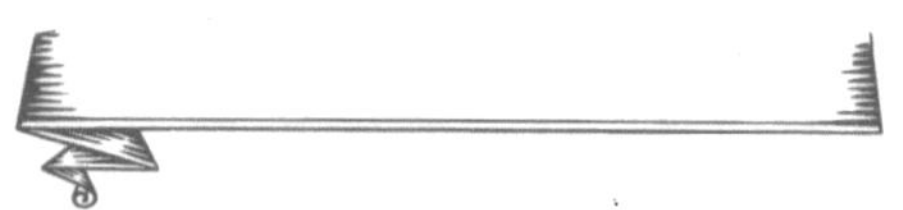

Preparing for competitive exams is a journey filled with both challenges and triumphs, but with the right mindset and approach, you can navigate it successfully. Here's how to prepare emotionally for the road ahead:

1. Set Clear Goals: Define your goals and aspirations clearly. Visualize the outcome you desire and let it fuel your motivation. Whether it's securing a coveted position or fulfilling a lifelong dream, keep your goals at the forefront of your mind as you embark on your preparation journey.

2. Create a Study Plan: Break down the vast syllabus into manageable chunks and create a study plan that works for you. Allocate time for each subject or topic, ensuring a balanced approach to your preparation. Remember, consistency is key, so stick to your plan and pace yourself accordingly.

3. Stay Organized: Keep track of study materials, resources, and important deadlines to avoid feeling overwhelmed. Organize your study space to minimize distractions and create an environment conducive to focused learning. A clutter-free space can help declutter your mind and enhance productivity.

4. Practice Self-Care: Prioritize self-care to maintain your physical, mental, and emotional well-being throughout your preparation. Get adequate rest, eat nourishing meals, and engage

in activities that relax and rejuvenate you. Remember, taking care of yourself is not a luxury but a necessity for success.

5. Stay Positive: Cultivate a positive mindset and believe in your abilities to overcome challenges. Replace negative thoughts with affirmations and reminders of your strengths. Surround yourself with positivity by seeking out supportive friends, mentors, or online communities who uplift and inspire you.

6. Seek Guidance: Don't hesitate to seek guidance from experienced mentors, teachers, or peers who can provide valuable insights and advice. Ask questions, clarify doubts, and leverage their expertise to enhance your understanding of difficult concepts. Remember, you're not alone on this journey – reach out for support when needed.

7. Practice Mindfulness: Incorporate mindfulness practices into your daily routine to stay grounded and focused. Take breaks to practice deep breathing, meditation, or visualization techniques that calm your mind and reduce stress. Mindfulness can help you stay present and attentive during your study sessions, improving concentration and retention.

8. Celebrate Small Wins: Celebrate your progress and accomplishments, no matter how small they may seem. Each milestone, whether mastering a challenging concept or completing a practice test, is a testament to your dedication and hard work. Acknowledge your efforts and reward yourself for your achievements along the way.

9. Stay Flexible: Be open to adapting your study strategies as needed based on your progress and feedback. Stay flexible and embrace change, whether it's adjusting your study schedule, trying new study techniques, or seeking alternative resources.

Adaptability is key to overcoming obstacles and finding effective solutions.

10. Believe in Yourself: Above all, believe in yourself and your ability to succeed. Trust in the resilience and determination that have brought you this far. Embrace the challenges as opportunities for growth and learning, knowing that each step forward brings you closer to your goals. You are capable, you are worthy, and you are destined for greatness – believe it with all your heart.

Preparing for competitive exams is not just about mastering content; it's about cultivating the resilience, determination, and self-belief needed to overcome obstacles and achieve your dreams. Embrace the journey with courage and conviction, knowing that every step forward brings you closer to the bright future that awaits you. You've got this!

1: Understanding the Competitive Exam Landscape

Competitive exams come in various shapes and sizes, each with its own set of rules, patterns, and expectations. Before diving into preparation, it's crucial to understand the landscape of the exams you're planning to take. This chapter will provide you with a comprehensive overview of different types of competitive exams, their formats, and the skills they assess.

Competitive exams can be broadly categorized into three main types: entrance exams, recruitment exams, and scholarship exams. Entrance exams are typically used for admission into educational institutions, such as colleges, universities, or specialized programs. Examples include the SAT, ACT, GRE, GMAT, and various national-level entrance exams like JEE, NEET, and CLAT.

Recruitment exams, on the other hand, are conducted by government agencies or private organizations to select candidates for job positions. These exams can range from civil services exams like UPSC and SSC to banking exams like IBPS and SBI PO, as well as exams for specific industries such as engineering, teaching, and healthcare.

Scholarship exams are designed to identify and reward talented students with financial assistance for their education.

These exams can be merit-based, need-based, or talent-based and are often conducted by educational institutions, government bodies, or private organizations.

Regardless of the type of exam, they all have certain common elements, including a syllabus, exam pattern, duration, and marking scheme. Understanding these elements is essential for effective preparation. For example, knowing the syllabus helps you identify the topics you need to cover, while understanding the exam pattern allows you to familiarize yourself with the types of questions asked and the time constraints you'll face.

In addition to understanding the exam format, it's also important to assess your strengths and weaknesses to develop a targeted preparation strategy. Take practice tests or diagnostic exams to identify areas where you need improvement and areas where you excel. This will help you allocate your time and resources more effectively during the preparation phase.

Overall, mastering competitive exams requires a combination of knowledge, skills, and strategic planning. By understanding the landscape of the exams you're preparing for, you can lay a strong foundation for success in your exam journey. In the following chapters, we'll delve deeper into specific strategies and techniques to help you maximize your performance and achieve your goals.

2: Setting SMART Goals for Success

Success in competitive exams is not just about working hard; it's also about working smart. And setting SMART goals is the first step towards a smart approach to exam preparation. In this chapter, we'll delve into the principles of SMART goal setting and how you can apply them to your exam preparation journey.

SMART is an acronym that stands for Specific, Measurable, Achievable, Relevant, and Time-bound. Let's break down each component:

1. Specific: Your goals should be clear and well-defined. Instead of setting a vague goal like "improve my math skills," make it specific by saying "score 80% or above in the math section of the exam." This clarity helps you focus your efforts and track your progress more effectively.

2. Measurable: Your goals should be quantifiable so that you can measure your progress and know when you've achieved them. Use metrics like scores, percentages, or completion deadlines to make your goals measurable. For example, "complete five practice tests with scores above 85%" is a measurable goal.

3. Achievable: While it's good to aim high, your goals should also be realistic and attainable. Consider your current abilities,

resources, and constraints when setting your goals. Setting unrealistic goals can lead to frustration and demotivation. Instead, set challenging yet achievable goals that push you out of your comfort zone without overwhelming you.

4. Relevant: Your goals should align with your overall objectives and priorities. They should be meaningful and relevant to your exam preparation journey. Avoid setting goals just for the sake of it; make sure they contribute to your ultimate success in the exam.

5. Time-bound: Every goal needs a deadline. Setting a timeframe creates a sense of urgency and helps you stay focused and disciplined. Break down your larger goals into smaller, manageable tasks with deadlines. For example, if your exam is six months away, set monthly or weekly goals to track your progress and stay on track.

Now that you understand the principles of SMART goal setting, it's time to apply them to your exam preparation. Start by identifying your long-term exam goals, such as the target score or rank you want to achieve. Then, break them down into smaller, actionable steps using the SMART criteria.

For instance, if your goal is to score 90% in the exam, your SMART goals could include:

- Specific: Review algebraic concepts and practice solving equations.

- Measurable: Complete ten algebra practice sets with scores above 85%.

- Achievable: Allocate two hours daily for algebra practice sessions.

- Relevant: Algebra is a significant portion of the exam syllabus.

- Time-bound: Complete all algebra practice sets within two weeks.

By setting SMART goals, you'll not only clarify your objectives but also increase your chances of success by making your goals actionable and achievable. Stay committed to your goals, track your progress regularly, and adjust your strategy as needed to stay on course towards exam success.

 K. AHRAM

Setting goals is the first step in turning the invisible into the visible." —Tony Robbins

3: Crafting an Effective Study Plan

Success in competitive exams requires more than just cramming information at the last minute. It demands a well-structured study plan that covers all aspects of the exam syllabus and allows for systematic preparation over time. In this chapter, we'll explore how to craft an effective study plan that maximizes your learning and minimizes stress.

1. Assess Your Strengths and Weaknesses: Before creating a study plan, it's essential to assess your current knowledge and skills. Identify your strengths, areas of improvement, and topics you find challenging. This self-assessment will help you allocate more time and resources to areas where you need the most improvement.

2. Set Realistic Goals: Building on the SMART goal-setting principles discussed earlier, set realistic goals for each study session, week, and month. Break down your exam syllabus into manageable chunks and assign specific topics or chapters to each study session. Make sure your goals are achievable within the timeframe you've set.

3. Create a Study Schedule: Once you've set your goals, create a study schedule that fits your lifestyle and commitments. Determine how many hours you can dedicate to studying each day and allocate time slots for different subjects or topics.

Consistency is key, so try to stick to your schedule as much as possible.

4. Prioritize High-Value Topics: Not all topics in the exam syllabus carry the same weightage. Identify high-value topics that are more likely to appear in the exam or contribute significantly to your overall score. Prioritize these topics in your study plan and allocate more time to mastering them.

5. Mix Up Your Study Methods: Variety is the spice of learning. Instead of sticking to one study method, mix it up to keep things interesting and maximize retention. Incorporate techniques like reading from textbooks, watching educational videos, solving practice questions, and discussing concepts with peers or mentors.

6. Include Regular Revision Sessions: Revision is crucial for long-term retention. Schedule regular revision sessions in your study plan to review previously covered material and reinforce your learning. Use spaced repetition techniques to ensure that you retain information effectively over time.

7. Stay Flexible and Adapt: While it's essential to stick to your study plan as much as possible, be flexible and willing to adapt as needed. Life is unpredictable, and unexpected events may disrupt your schedule from time to time. Instead of getting discouraged, adjust your plan accordingly and make up for lost time when possible.

8. Take Breaks and Practice Self-Care: Remember to take regular breaks during study sessions to avoid burnout and maintain productivity. Practice self-care activities like exercise, meditation, and adequate sleep to keep your mind and body in top condition for optimal learning.

By following these steps, you can craft an effective study plan that sets you up for success in your competitive exams. Remember that consistency, dedication, and smart planning are the keys to achieving your goals. Stay focused, stay motivated, and keep pushing forward towards exam success.

"In the midst of challenges, remember the strength within you, waiting to be unleashed like a roaring lion. Embrace the journey, for every obstacle is a stepping stone to greatness. Let determination be your compass, guiding you through the darkest of nights. With every setback, let resilience be your armor, shielding you from doubt's cruel arrows. Believe in the power of your dreams, for they are the stars that light your path. And remember, dear student, that the journey may be long, but the destination is worth every trial endured. So rise, shine, and conquer the world with your brilliance."

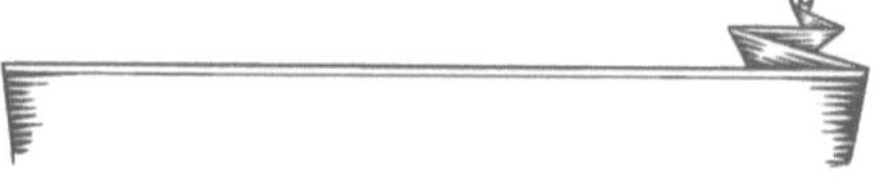

4: Mastering Time Management Techniques

Effective time management is a cornerstone of successful exam preparation. With a limited amount of time available, it's essential to make the most of every minute and prioritize tasks strategically. In this chapter, we'll explore various time management techniques and strategies to help you optimize your study schedule and maximize productivity.

1. Set Priorities: Start by identifying your high-priority tasks and goals for each study session or day. Focus on the topics or areas that require immediate attention or contribute most significantly to your exam performance. By setting clear priorities, you can ensure that you allocate your time and energy wisely.

2. Use the Pomodoro Technique: The Pomodoro Technique is a time management method that involves breaking your study time into intervals, typically 25 minutes long, separated by short breaks. During each interval, focus exclusively on studying, then take a short break to rest and recharge. This technique can help improve concentration and productivity by preventing burnout and maintaining focus.

3. Create a Study Schedule: Develop a detailed study schedule that allocates specific time slots for different subjects

or topics based on their importance and your proficiency level. Include breaks, meals, and other non-study activities in your schedule to maintain balance and prevent fatigue. Stick to your schedule as much as possible, but be flexible and adjust as needed.

4. Use Time Blocking: Time blocking involves dividing your day into blocks of time dedicated to specific tasks or activities. Allocate dedicated blocks of time for studying, revising, practicing, and other essential tasks related to exam preparation. This approach helps you stay organized, focused, and on track with your study goals.

5. Eliminate Distractions: Identify and eliminate distractions that may hinder your productivity during study sessions. Turn off notifications on your phone, close unnecessary tabs on your computer, and create a quiet, distraction-free study environment. Minimize interruptions and focus solely on the task at hand to make the most of your study time.

6. Break Tasks into Smaller Steps: Break down larger study tasks or projects into smaller, manageable steps to make them less overwhelming and more achievable. This approach helps prevent procrastination and allows you to make steady progress towards your goals. Celebrate small victories along the way to stay motivated and maintain momentum.

7. Use Time Management Tools: Leverage technology and time management tools to help you stay organized and on track with your study schedule. Use apps, calendars, or task management tools to plan your study sessions, set reminders, and track your progress. Experiment with different tools to find what works best for you.

8. Review and Reflect: At the end of each study day or week, take time to review your progress, reflect on what worked well, and identify areas for improvement. Adjust your study schedule and techniques accordingly based on your observations and feedback. Continuous reflection and adaptation are key to refining your time management skills and optimizing your study routine.

By implementing these time management techniques and strategies, you can make the most of your study time, increase your productivity, and achieve better results in your competitive exams. Remember that effective time management is a skill that can be developed and refined over time with practice and perseverance.

"Success usually comes to those who are too busy to be looking for it." —Henry David Thoreau

5: Strategies for Effective Note-taking and Revision

Taking effective notes and revising them systematically are essential components of successful exam preparation. In this chapter, we'll delve into strategies to enhance your note-taking skills and make the most out of your revision sessions.

1. Active Listening and Engagement: During lectures, classes, or study sessions, actively engage with the material by listening attentively, asking questions, and participating in discussions. Actively engaging with the material helps improve understanding and retention, making note-taking more effective.

2. Choose the Right Note-taking Method: There are various note-taking methods, such as the Cornell method, outlining, mind mapping, and the SQ3R method. Experiment with different methods to find the one that works best for you and suits the type of content you're studying.

3. Organize Your Notes Effectively: Keep your notes organized and structured for easy reference and review. Use headings, bullet points, and numbering to break down information into digestible chunks. Color coding or

highlighting important points can also help enhance organization and retrieval.

4. Focus on Key Concepts and Keywords: Instead of transcribing everything word-for-word, focus on capturing key concepts, ideas, and keywords during note-taking. Summarize information in your own words, and use abbreviations or symbols to save time and space.

5. Review and Revise Your Notes Regularly: Schedule regular review sessions to revisit your notes and reinforce your learning. Use active recall techniques, such as self-quizzing or explaining concepts to yourself or others, to test your understanding and retention. Reviewing your notes regularly helps transfer information from short-term to long-term memory.

6. Create Summary Sheets or Flashcards: Condense your notes into summary sheets or flashcards for quick and efficient revision. Highlight key points, formulas, and definitions, and use mnemonic devices or acronyms to aid memorization. Flashcards are particularly effective for rote memorization and self-assessment.

7. Utilize Technology for Note-taking and Revision: Take advantage of technology tools and apps for digital note-taking and revision. Use note-taking apps like Evernote or OneNote to organize and sync your notes across devices. Explore spaced repetition apps like Anki for efficient flashcard-based revision.

8. Teach and Discuss with Peers: Teaching others or discussing concepts with peers can deepen your understanding and reinforce your learning. Organize study groups or tutoring sessions where you can share and explain your notes to others, and benefit from their insights and explanations.

9. Seek Feedback and Adjust: Solicit feedback on your notes from teachers, mentors, or peers, and use it to improve and refine your note-taking approach. Pay attention to areas where your notes may be unclear or incomplete, and make adjustments accordingly.

By implementing these strategies for effective note-taking and revision, you can enhance your study efficiency, improve your retention of information, and boost your performance in competitive exams. Remember that note-taking is not just about capturing information but also about actively engaging with and processing the material for deeper understanding and retention.

"There is no wealth like knowledge, no poverty like ignorance".__
Ali ibn abi Talib

6: Enhancing Memory and Retention Skills

A strong memory is a valuable asset when it comes to exam preparation. In this chapter, we'll explore techniques and strategies to enhance your memory and retention skills, helping you remember important information more effectively.

1. Practice Retrieval: The act of recalling information from memory strengthens neural pathways and enhances retention. Incorporate regular retrieval practice into your study routine by actively recalling facts, concepts, and formulas without referring to your notes. This can include self-quizzing, flashcards, or simply trying to recall information from memory.

2. Use Spaced Repetition: Spaced repetition is a scientifically proven technique that involves reviewing information at increasing intervals over time. Utilize spaced repetition software or apps like Anki to create flashcards and schedule review sessions based on your learning progress. This method optimizes memory retention by spacing out review sessions at optimal intervals.

3. Create Mnemonics and Memory Aids: Mnemonics are memory aids or techniques that help you remember information more easily by associating it with vivid imagery, acronyms, or rhymes. Create mnemonic devices for complex concepts,

formulas, or lists to make them more memorable and easier to recall during exams.

4. Chunking Information: Chunking involves breaking down large amounts of information into smaller, more manageable chunks. Group related information together and organize it into meaningful patterns or categories. This helps reduce cognitive load and makes it easier to process and remember the information.

5. Visualize Concepts: Visual imagery can be a powerful tool for memory retention. Try to visualize concepts, processes, or relationships in your mind's eye to create mental images that are easier to remember. Use diagrams, charts, or mind maps to represent information visually and aid comprehension and recall.

6. Associate Information with Personal Experiences: Relating new information to personal experiences, stories, or anecdotes can make it more meaningful and memorable. Draw connections between abstract concepts and real-life examples to anchor the information in your memory and facilitate recall.

7. Get Sufficient Sleep: Adequate sleep is essential for memory consolidation and retention. Aim for 7-9 hours of quality sleep each night to allow your brain to process and store information effectively. Avoid cramming late into the night before exams, as sleep deprivation can impair memory and cognitive function.

8. Stay Physically Active: Regular physical exercise has been shown to enhance cognitive function and memory. Incorporate physical activity into your daily routine to improve blood flow to the brain and promote the growth of new neurons. Even short

bursts of exercise can have a positive impact on memory and learning.

9. Practice Mindfulness and Meditation: Mindfulness and meditation techniques can help improve focus, attention, and memory retention. Dedicate time each day to mindfulness practices such as deep breathing, meditation, or yoga to reduce stress, enhance concentration, and improve overall cognitive function.

By incorporating these memory-enhancing techniques into your study routine, you can boost your ability to retain and recall information, ultimately improving your performance in competitive exams. Remember that memory is like a muscle that can be trained and strengthened with practice and persistence.

"Success is getting what you want; happiness is wanting what you get."—W. P. Kinsella

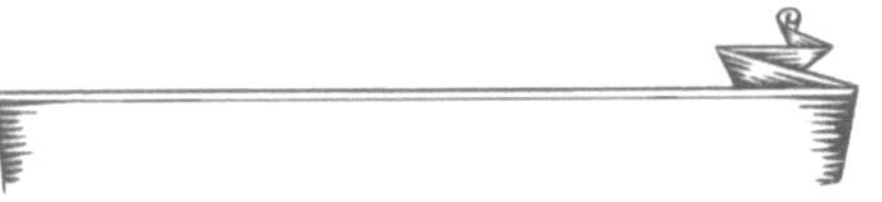

7: Practicing with Mock Tests and Sample Papers

Mock tests and sample papers are invaluable tools for exam preparation, offering opportunities to assess your knowledge, familiarize yourself with the exam format, and identify areas for improvement. In this chapter, we'll explore how to make the most of mock tests and sample papers to enhance your exam readiness.

1. Simulate Exam Conditions: When taking mock tests or practicing with sample papers, simulate exam conditions as closely as possible. Choose a quiet, distraction-free environment, set a timer to mimic the exam duration, and adhere to the exam rules and guidelines. Practicing under realistic conditions helps reduce test-day anxiety and improves your ability to perform under pressure.

2. Cover a Range of Topics: Select mock tests and sample papers that cover a diverse range of topics and question types relevant to your exam syllabus. This ensures that you're adequately prepared for any question that may appear on the actual exam. Prioritize topics based on their importance and your proficiency level.

3. Analyze Your Performance: After completing a mock test or sample paper, thoroughly analyze your performance to

identify strengths and weaknesses. Review each question to understand why you got it right or wrong, and pinpoint areas where you need improvement. Pay attention to recurring patterns or types of questions that you struggle with.

4. Review Answer Explanations: Many mock tests and sample papers provide answer explanations or solutions for each question. Take advantage of these resources to deepen your understanding of concepts and learn from your mistakes. Reviewing answer explanations helps clarify misconceptions, reinforce learning, and improve future performance.

5. Track Your Progress: Keep track of your mock test scores and performance over time to monitor your progress and identify trends. Note any improvements or areas where you're consistently struggling, and adjust your study plan accordingly. Tracking your progress provides valuable feedback and helps you stay motivated and focused on your goals.

6. Simulate Time Management: Practice managing your time effectively during mock tests by allocating a specific amount of time to each section or question. If you find yourself running out of time, reassess your time allocation strategy and practice pacing yourself more efficiently. Time management is crucial for completing the exam within the allotted time constraints.

7. Iterate and Improve: Use mock tests and sample papers as opportunities for continuous improvement. Incorporate feedback from your performance analyses, adjust your study strategies, and iterate on your approach to tackling different types of questions. The goal is not just to practice, but to learn from each practice session and become more proficient over time.

8. Seek Feedback and Guidance: If you're struggling to improve your performance or address specific challenges, seek feedback and guidance from teachers, mentors, or peers. They can provide valuable insights, tips, and strategies to help you overcome obstacles and excel in your exam preparation.

By incorporating mock tests and sample papers into your study routine, you can identify areas for improvement, refine your exam-taking skills, and increase your confidence and readiness for the actual exam. Treat each mock test as an opportunity to learn and grow, and leverage the insights gained to enhance your overall exam performance.

"I never dreamed about success. I worked for it." —Estée Lauder

8: Analyzing and Learning from Mistakes

Mistakes are an inevitable part of the learning process, and how you respond to them can greatly influence your progress and success in exam preparation. In this chapter, we'll explore the importance of analyzing mistakes and strategies for turning them into opportunities for learning and growth.

1. Embrace a Growth Mindset: Adopt a growth mindset, which views mistakes as opportunities for learning and improvement rather than signs of failure. Understand that making mistakes is a natural part of the learning process and an essential step towards mastery.

2. Review Mistakes Thoroughly: When you encounter a mistake, whether it's in a practice test, homework assignment, or study session, take the time to review it thoroughly. Identify the root cause of the mistake, whether it was a conceptual misunderstanding, a calculation error, or a lack of attention to detail.

3. Understand Why the Mistake Occurred: Dig deeper to understand why the mistake occurred. Was it due to a lack of understanding of the underlying concept? Did you misinterpret the question? Were you rushing or under pressure? By

pinpointing the cause of the mistake, you can address the underlying issue and prevent similar errors in the future.

4. Seek Feedback: If you're unsure about why you made a particular mistake, seek feedback from teachers, tutors, or peers. They can provide insights and explanations that help clarify your understanding and identify areas for improvement.

5. Correct Misconceptions: Use mistakes as opportunities to correct any misconceptions or misunderstandings you may have about the material. Consult textbooks, online resources, or additional study materials to gain a deeper understanding of the concept or topic in question.

6. Create a Mistake Log: Keep a mistake log or journal where you record the mistakes you make during your study sessions or practice tests. Write down the nature of the mistake, the context in which it occurred, and what you learned from it. Reviewing your mistake log regularly helps track patterns, monitor progress, and reinforce learning.

7. Implement Corrective Action: Once you've analyzed a mistake and identified the underlying cause, take corrective action to address it. This may involve relearning the concept, practicing similar problems, or adjusting your study strategies to prevent similar mistakes in the future.

8. Practice Deliberate Practice: Engage in deliberate practice, which involves focused and intentional practice aimed at improving specific skills or addressing weaknesses. Target areas where you tend to make mistakes and practice them systematically until you achieve mastery.

9. Stay Positive and Persistent: Maintain a positive attitude towards mistakes and setbacks, recognizing them as opportunities for growth and improvement. Stay persistent in

your efforts to learn from your mistakes and continue pushing forward towards your goals.

By embracing mistakes as opportunities for learning and growth, you can turn setbacks into stepping stones towards success in your exam preparation. Remember that the journey to mastery is not always smooth, but by analyzing and learning from your mistakes, you can become a more resilient, knowledgeable, and confident learner.

"Develop success from failures. Discouragement and failure are two of the surest stepping stones to success." —Dale Carnegie

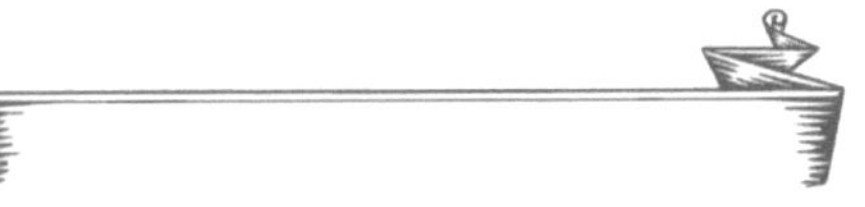

9 : Improving Speed and Accuracy in Problem Solving

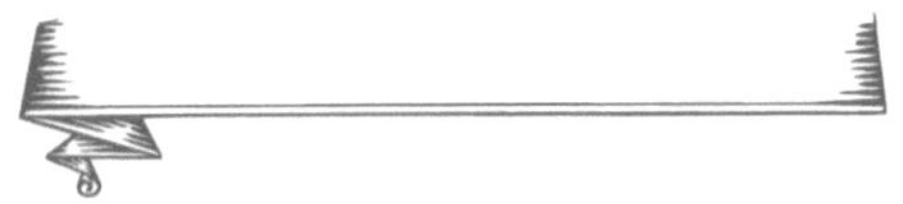

Improving speed and accuracy in problem-solving is paramount when preparing for competitive exams, as it directly influences success rates and overall performance. Competitive exams are designed to assess a candidate's ability to think critically, solve complex problems, and make quick decisions under pressure. Whether it's an entrance exam for a prestigious university, a standardized test for professional certification, or a competitive job placement exam, candidates must navigate through a myriad of questions within a limited time frame. Hence, mastering the art of problem-solving with precision and efficiency becomes indispensable. There are several strategies and techniques one can employ to enhance their speed and accuracy in problem-solving, each rooted in understanding the nature of the exam, practicing consistently, and adopting effective time-management skills.

Firstly, familiarizing oneself with the exam format and question types is crucial. By understanding the structure of the exam, candidates can tailor their preparation methods accordingly. This involves analyzing past papers, identifying recurring patterns, and pinpointing areas of strength and weakness. For instance, if a particular exam heavily emphasizes mathematical reasoning, candidates can allocate more time to practicing mathematical problems and honing their numerical skills. Similarly, if the exam includes sections on verbal reasoning or logical deduction, candidates can focus on enhancing their comprehension and analytical abilities in those domains. Moreover, becoming acquainted with shortcuts, formulas, and problem-solving techniques specific to the exam can significantly expedite the solving process.

Secondly, consistent practice is key to improving speed and accuracy in problem-solving. Regular practice not only reinforces concepts and techniques but also builds confidence and familiarity with different question formats. Devoting dedicated study sessions to solving problems under timed conditions simulates the pressure of the actual exam, enabling candidates to develop a rhythm and pace that suits them best. Additionally, practicing with a variety of difficulty levels ensures that candidates are prepared to tackle any challenge that may arise during the exam. This iterative process of learning from mistakes, refining strategies, and pushing one's limits is instrumental in achieving mastery in problem-solving.

Furthermore, adopting effective time-management strategies can significantly enhance one's performance in competitive exams. Time is a precious resource during exams, and allocating it judiciously can make the difference between success and failure. One effective approach is to divide the allotted time for each section based on the number of questions and their complexity. By setting time targets for individual questions or passages, candidates can prioritize their efforts and avoid getting bogged down by challenging problems. Additionally, learning to recognize when to skip a question and come back to it later can prevent wasting valuable time on a single unsolvable problem. Moreover, practicing mental math and quick estimation techniques can expedite calculations and reduce reliance on lengthy pen-and-paper methods.

Another crucial aspect of improving speed and accuracy in problem-solving is maintaining focus and concentration throughout the exam. Distractions, anxiety, and fatigue can impair cognitive function and hinder performance. Therefore, adopting mindfulness techniques such as deep breathing, positive visualization, and periodic breaks can help candidates stay calm and centered during the exam. Additionally, cultivating a healthy lifestyle through adequate sleep, nutritious diet, and regular exercise can enhance cognitive function and mental alertness, thereby boosting problem-solving abilities.

In conclusion, improving speed and accuracy in problem-solving is essential for success in competitive exams. By understanding the exam format, practicing consistently, adopting effective time-management strategies, and maintaining focus and concentration, candidates can optimize their performance and maximize their chances of achieving their desired outcomes. Ultimately, mastery in problem-solving is not merely about finding the right answers but also about doing so efficiently and confidently within the constraints of time and pressure.

Moreover, leveraging technology can further augment one's ability to solve problems swiftly and accurately. Utilizing online resources, such as practice tests, interactive tutorials, and educational apps, provides candidates with a dynamic and adaptive learning environment. These tools offer instant feedback, personalized recommendations, and real-time performance analytics, enabling candidates to identify areas for improvement and track their progress over time. Additionally, incorporating digital platforms for collaborative learning, such as forums, study groups, and virtual classrooms, facilitates knowledge sharing and peer support, fostering a sense of community and motivation among aspirants.

Furthermore, cultivating a growth mindset is instrumental in overcoming obstacles and continually striving for improvement in problem-solving skills. Embracing challenges, viewing failures as opportunities for learning, and maintaining a positive attitude towards self-improvement are hallmark traits of individuals with a growth mindset. By reframing setbacks as stepping stones to success and persisting in the face of adversity, candidates can build resilience and confidence in their problem-solving abilities. Additionally, seeking guidance from mentors, teachers, or experienced professionals can provide valuable insights, strategies, and encouragement to navigate the complexities of competitive exams effectively.

Additionally, staying updated with current affairs, emerging trends, and recent developments in relevant fields can enrich one's problem-solving repertoire and enhance overall performance in competitive exams. Many exams include sections on general knowledge, current affairs, and critical reasoning, which require candidates to apply their problem-solving skills in real-world contexts. By staying abreast of global events, technological advancements, and socio-economic trends, candidates can broaden their perspectives, sharpen their analytical abilities, and approach problems from diverse angles. Moreover, cultivating a habit of lifelong learning through reading, attending workshops, and participating in discussions fosters intellectual curiosity and expands one's knowledge base, thereby equipping candidates with a competitive edge in exams and beyond.

In conclusion, improving speed and accuracy in problem-solving is a multifaceted endeavor that requires a combination of knowledge, skills, and mindset. By leveraging exam-specific strategies, practicing consistently, managing time effectively, maintaining focus and concentration, utilizing technology, cultivating a growth mindset, and staying updated with current affairs, candidates can enhance their problem-solving abilities and excel in competitive exams. Ultimately, success in competitive exams is not solely determined by innate talent or intelligence but rather by one's ability to adapt, persevere, and continuously strive for excellence in problem-solving.

10: CONSISTENCY

In the grand tapestry of life, consistency emerges as the golden thread that weaves dreams into reality. Nowhere is its importance more profound than in the realm of preparing for competitive exams, where every moment, every effort, holds the power to shape destinies and carve paths towards success. Consistency, like the steady rhythm of a heartbeat, sustains the fervor of aspiration and fuels the fires of determination, guiding aspirants through the labyrinth of challenges towards the coveted prize of triumph.

Picture the journey of a determined soul embarking upon the path of preparation for a competitive exam. At the outset, the vision is crystal clear, the passion ablaze with the fervent desire to conquer the heights of achievement. With each dawn, they arise with renewed vigor, eager to seize the day and inch closer to their aspirations. In the early stages, the journey may seem like a sprint, fueled by adrenaline and enthusiasm, but soon they realize that victory is not won by momentary bursts of brilliance, but by the steady march of consistency.

Consistency is the silent guardian that stands unwavering amidst the tempests of doubt and uncertainty. It is the beacon of hope that illuminates the darkest of nights, guiding aspirants through the labyrinth of challenges and setbacks. When the weight of expectations threatens to crush their spirit and the specter of failure looms large on the horizon, it is consistency that lends them the strength to persevere, to rise from the ashes of defeat, and to forge ahead with unwavering resolve.

Moreover, consistency breeds confidence, transforming timid whispers of self-doubt into resounding echoes of self-assurance. As aspirants adhere steadfastly to their study schedules, investing time and effort into honing their skills and mastering their craft, they begin to witness the fruits of their labor blooming before their very eyes. Each incremental improvement, each milestone achieved, serves as a testament to the power of consistency, emboldening them to push past their limits and reach for the stars.

Yet, consistency is not merely about maintaining a rigid routine or adhering blindly to a predetermined plan. It is a dynamic force that adapts and evolves with the ebb and flow of life's currents. There will be days when the winds of adversity blow fiercely, threatening to derail even the most steadfast of aspirations. In such moments, it is important to remember that consistency is not synonymous with perfection. It is about showing up, day in and day out, even when the road ahead seems daunting and the odds are stacked against you.

In the grand tapestry of life, consistency emerges as the golden thread that weaves dreams into reality. Nowhere is its importance more profound than in the realm of preparing for competitive exams, where every moment, every effort, holds the power to shape destinies and carve paths towards success. Consistency, like the steady rhythm of a heartbeat, sustains the fervor of aspiration and fuels the fires of determination, guiding aspirants through the labyrinth of challenges towards the coveted prize of triumph.

Picture the journey of a determined soul embarking upon the path of preparation for a competitive exam. At the outset, the vision is crystal clear, the passion ablaze with the fervent desire to conquer the heights of achievement. With each dawn, they arise with renewed vigor, eager to seize the day and inch closer to their aspirations. In the early stages, the journey may seem like a sprint, fueled by adrenaline and enthusiasm, but soon they realize that victory is not won by momentary bursts of brilliance, but by the steady march of consistency.

Consistency is the silent guardian that stands unwavering amidst the tempests of doubt and uncertainty. It is the beacon of hope that illuminates the darkest of nights, guiding aspirants through the labyrinth of challenges and setbacks. When the weight of expectations threatens to crush their spirit and the specter of failure looms large on the horizon, it is consistency that lends them the strength to persevere, to rise from the ashes of defeat, and to forge ahead with unwavering resolve.

Moreover, consistency breeds confidence, transforming timid whispers of self-doubt into resounding echoes of self-assurance. As aspirants adhere steadfastly to their study schedules, investing time and effort into honing their skills and mastering their craft, they begin to witness the fruits of their labor blooming before their very eyes. Each incremental improvement, each milestone achieved, serves as a testament to the power of consistency, emboldening them to push past their limits and reach for the stars.

Yet, consistency is not merely about maintaining a rigid routine or adhering blindly to a predetermined plan. It is a dynamic force that adapts and evolves with the ebb and flow of life's currents. There will be days when the winds of adversity blow fiercely, threatening to derail even the most steadfast of aspirations. In such moments, it is important to remember that consistency is not synonymous with perfection. It is about showing up, day in and day out, even when the road ahead seems daunting and the odds are stacked against you.

In the face of adversity, consistency serves as a lifeline, anchoring aspirants to their goals and reminding them of the unwavering commitment they have made to themselves. It is the steady hand that steadies their trembling resolve and the gentle whisper that urges them to keep moving forward, one step at a time. With each passing day, as they continue to show up and put in the work, they inch closer towards their dreams, fueled by the unshakeable belief that consistency is the key to unlocking the doors of opportunity and ushering them into a future filled with boundless possibilities.

Moreover, consistency is the hallmark of champions, separating the ordinary from the extraordinary. It is the secret ingredient that transforms fleeting moments of brilliance into enduring legacies of greatness. History is replete with examples of individuals who, through unwavering consistency and relentless perseverance, have transcended the limitations of circumstance and rewritten the script of their own destiny. Whether it be the athlete who trains tirelessly in the pursuit of Olympic glory or the scholar who burns the midnight oil in search of academic excellence, their stories serve as a testament to the transformative power of consistency in the pursuit of greatness.

Yet, perhaps the greatest gift of consistency lies not in the trophies won or the accolades earned, but in the journey itself. For it is through the daily grind, the relentless pursuit of progress, that aspirants discover the true measure of their strength and the depths of their resilience. It is in the moments of struggle and adversity that they forge bonds of camaraderie and solidarity, drawing strength from the shared pursuit of a common goal. And it is in the quiet moments of reflection, as they look back on how far they have come, that they realize the profound truth that consistency is not just a means to an end, but a way of life.

In conclusion, the importance of consistency while preparing for competitive exams cannot be overstated. It is the bedrock upon which dreams are built and the fuel that propels aspirants towards their goals. Through unwavering commitment and relentless perseverance, consistency transforms aspirations into achievements and ordinary individuals into champions. So, as you embark upon the journey of preparation, remember that success is not a destination to be reached, but a journey to be embraced. And in that journey, let consistency be your steadfast companion, guiding you through the trials and tribulations towards the pinnacle of triumph.

11: Staying Motivated Throughout the Preparation Journey

Staying motivated throughout the preparation journey for competitive exams is paramount for achieving success in the face of challenges and uncertainties. The journey towards such exams is often long and arduous, requiring dedication, perseverance, and a resilient mindset. Maintaining motivation becomes the cornerstone of this journey, fueling the drive to push through obstacles and stay focused on the ultimate goal of success.

First and foremost, understanding the "why" behind your pursuit is crucial. Clarifying your motivations, whether it's personal fulfillment, career advancement, or a sense of achievement, provides a solid foundation to anchor your efforts. Knowing the significance of the exam in relation to your aspirations can help sustain your enthusiasm even during the toughest times. Moreover, visualizing the rewards and opportunities that await upon successful completion of the exam can serve as a powerful source of inspiration, reminding you of the ultimate prize that lies ahead.

Equally important is cultivating a positive mindset and adopting effective strategies to stay motivated. Breaking down the preparation process into manageable tasks and setting realistic goals can prevent overwhelm and instill a sense of progress and accomplishment along the way. Celebrating small victories, whether it's mastering a difficult concept or improving performance in mock tests, reinforces a sense of competence and boosts morale. Additionally, surrounding yourself with a supportive network of friends, family, mentors, or study partners can provide encouragement and accountability, helping you stay on track even when motivation wanes.

Furthermore, maintaining a healthy work-life balance is essential for sustaining motivation in the long run. Prioritizing self-care activities such as exercise, adequate sleep, and relaxation not only rejuvenates your mind and body but also enhances focus and productivity during study sessions. Taking regular breaks to recharge and indulge in hobbies or interests outside of exam preparation prevents burnout and maintains overall well-being. Remember, the journey towards success is not just about the destination but also about the experiences and growth gained along the way.

In addition to internal motivation, external sources of inspiration can also play a significant role in keeping you motivated throughout the preparation journey. Drawing inspiration from role models or success stories of individuals who have overcome similar challenges and achieved their goals can instill belief in your own capabilities and reinforce the notion that success is attainable with dedication and perseverance. Engaging with motivational resources such as books, podcasts, or motivational speakers can provide a constant source of encouragement and perspective, especially during moments of doubt or uncertainty.

Moreover, embracing failure as a natural part of the learning process and an opportunity for growth is essential for maintaining motivation during challenging times. Viewing setbacks as learning experiences rather than insurmountable obstacles cultivates resilience and adaptability, empowering you to bounce back stronger and more determined than before. Remember that setbacks are not indicative of your worth or potential but rather stepping stones towards eventual success.

Ultimately, staying motivated throughout the preparation journey for competitive exams is a combination of intrinsic passion, effective strategies, and a resilient mindset. By understanding your motivations, adopting positive habits, seeking inspiration from both internal and external sources, and embracing failure as a catalyst for growth, you can navigate the ups and downs of the journey with confidence and determination. With unwavering commitment and perseverance, success becomes not just a destination but a journey of self-discovery and personal growth.

Moreover, staying focused on the bigger picture and maintaining a sense of perspective is essential when facing challenges or setbacks. It's easy to get bogged down by temporary obstacles or minor setbacks, but keeping sight of the ultimate goal can help put things into perspective and renew your motivation. Remind yourself of the reasons why you embarked on this journey in the first place and the long-term benefits that await you upon successful completion of the exam. Whether it's advancing your career, pursuing your passions, or realizing your dreams, keeping your eyes on the prize can reignite your determination and propel you forward, even in the face of adversity.

Additionally, cultivating a growth mindset is crucial for staying motivated throughout the preparation journey. Embrace the belief that your abilities and intelligence are not fixed but can be developed through effort, perseverance, and learning from mistakes. By viewing challenges as opportunities for growth and setbacks as temporary roadblocks rather than permanent failures, you empower yourself to overcome obstacles with resilience and optimism. Cultivating a growth mindset not only fuels motivation but also fosters a lifelong love of learning and personal development, setting the stage for continued success beyond the exam.

Furthermore, staying organized and maintaining a structured study plan can help alleviate feelings of overwhelm and ensure consistent progress towards your goals. Break down the syllabus into manageable chunks and create a realistic study schedule that accommodates your other commitments and allows for adequate rest and relaxation. Setting specific, measurable, achievable, relevant, and time-bound (SMART) goals can provide clarity and direction, guiding your efforts towards meaningful milestones and keeping you accountable along the way. Regularly review and adjust your study plan as needed to stay on track and adapt to changing circumstances, but remain flexible and compassionate with yourself during moments of difficulty or setbacks.

In conclusion, staying motivated throughout the preparation journey for competitive exams requires a combination of intrinsic passion, effective strategies, and a resilient mindset. By understanding your motivations, maintaining a positive attitude, seeking inspiration from internal and external sources, embracing failure as a learning opportunity, staying focused on the bigger picture, cultivating a growth mindset, and staying organized with a structured study plan, you can navigate the ups and downs of the journey with confidence and determination. Remember that success is not just about the destination but also about the growth, resilience, and personal development gained along the way. With dedication, perseverance, and a steadfast commitment to your goals, you can overcome any challenge and realize your full potential.

"In the dance of life, motivation and discipline are the twin stars guiding our steps through the dark night of uncertainty. Like flames flickering in the wind, they illuminate our path, casting shadows of doubt into the abyss. Motivation, a spark igniting the fire within, whispers promises of dreams yet to be realized, while discipline, the steady hand that molds our actions, shapes our aspirations into reality. Together, they orchestrate the symphony of our existence, weaving melodies of perseverance and determination into the fabric of our souls. For without them, we are but lost wanderers in a world devoid of purpose and direction."

12: HOW TO USE AI

Using AI for competitive exam preparation can significantly enhance efficiency and effectiveness. Here are several ways AI can be leveraged:

1. Personalized Learning Paths: AI algorithms can analyze the strengths and weaknesses of individual learners through diagnostic tests or by tracking their performance. Based on this analysis, personalized study plans can be generated, focusing on areas that need improvement while reinforcing strengths.

2. Adaptive Practice Tests: AI-powered platforms can offer adaptive practice tests that adjust difficulty levels based on the user's performance. This ensures that learners are continually challenged at an appropriate level, optimizing their preparation.

3. Content Recommendation: AI algorithms can recommend relevant study materials, resources, and practice questions based on the exam syllabus and the learner's preferences. This helps learners access high-quality content tailored to their needs.

4. Natural Language Processing (NLP) for Conceptual Understanding: NLP techniques can be used to extract key concepts from study materials, question papers, and explanations. AI-powered tools can then provide detailed

explanations, summaries, and concept maps to aid in conceptual understanding.

5. Question Answering Systems: AI-powered question answering systems can assist learners in understanding complex concepts by answering their queries in real-time. These systems can provide explanations, examples, and additional resources to clarify doubts.

6. Flashcards and Spaced Repetition: AI algorithms can optimize the use of flashcards and spaced repetition techniques to help learners memorize and retain information effectively. By scheduling review sessions based on the forgetting curve, AI ensures that learners revisit concepts at the right intervals for maximum retention.

7. Performance Analytics and Insights: AI-powered dashboards can provide learners with detailed analytics and insights into their performance, progress, and areas for improvement. Visualizations such as progress charts, skill matrices, and comparative analysis can motivate learners and help them track their growth.

8. Virtual Tutoring and Mentoring: AI-powered chatbots or virtual tutors can offer personalized guidance, support, and mentoring to learners round the clock. These virtual assistants can answer queries, provide explanations, offer study tips, and motivate learners throughout their preparation journey.

9. Gamification and Interactive Learning: AI can gamify the learning experience by incorporating elements such as badges, points, leaderboards, and simulations. Gamification not only makes learning more engaging but also encourages healthy competition among learners, motivating them to strive for improvement.

10. Predictive Analytics for Performance Forecasting: AI algorithms can analyze past exam data, learner performance trends, and various other factors to predict future performance. This helps learners set realistic goals, identify areas of focus, and strategize their preparation accordingly.

By integrating these AI-powered tools and techniques into competitive exam preparation, learners can enjoy a more personalized, engaging, and effective learning experience, ultimately enhancing their chances of success.

^HOPE FOR THE BEST PREPARE FOR WROST

13: SETBACKS

^ In life, when you've lost everything, that means you have nothing else to lose. From then, everything around you is available for you to gain.

Preparing for setbacks during your competitive exam journey is like equipping yourself with armor for battle. Here's how you can fortify yourself emotionally:

1. Anticipate Challenges: Understand that setbacks are a natural part of any journey, especially one as challenging as preparing for competitive exams. Expecting hurdles along the way prepares you to face them with resilience and determination.

2. Embrace a Growth Mindset: Instead of viewing setbacks as failures, see them as opportunities for growth and learning. Every setback is a chance to identify weaknesses, refine your strategies, and come back stronger than before.

3. Practice Self-Compassion: Be gentle with yourself when setbacks occur. Avoid self-blame or harsh criticism. Instead, offer yourself kindness and understanding, recognizing that setbacks are not a reflection of your worth or abilities.

4. Seek Support: Lean on your support system – friends, family, mentors, or peers – during challenging times. Sharing your struggles with others can provide valuable perspective,

encouragement, and emotional support to help you navigate setbacks.

5. Reflect and Adapt: Take time to reflect on what led to the setback and identify areas for improvement. Adjust your study strategies, time management techniques, or mindset as needed to overcome obstacles and continue making progress.

6. Stay Focused on Your Goals: Remind yourself of the bigger picture and why you embarked on this journey in the first place. Keep your goals in sight, and let them motivate you to persevere through setbacks and obstacles.

7. Practice Resilience-Building Activities: Engage in activities that strengthen your resilience and mental fortitude, such as mindfulness meditation, journaling, or physical exercise. These practices can help you bounce back from setbacks with renewed determination and positivity.

8. Celebrate Progress: Even in the face of setbacks, acknowledge the progress you've made so far. Celebrate small victories and milestones along the way, no matter how insignificant they may seem. Recognizing your achievements boosts your confidence and morale.

9. Maintain Perspective: Remember that setbacks are temporary roadblocks, not dead ends. Keep the bigger picture in mind and maintain a long-term perspective on your journey. Visualize yourself overcoming challenges and emerging victorious in the end.

10. Stay Flexible and Adaptable: Be open to adjusting your plans and expectations as circumstances change. Flexibility and adaptability are key traits for navigating setbacks and finding alternative paths to success.

Above all, believe in yourself and your ability to overcome any obstacle that comes your way. With resilience, perseverance, and a positive mindset, you can weather the storms of setbacks and emerge stronger on the other side. You've got this!

یہ حادثات نہ سمجھیں ابھی کہ پست ہوں میں شکستہ ہو کے بھی ناقابل شکست ہوں میں

متاعِ درد سے دل مالا مال ہے میرا زمانہ کیوں یہ سمجھتا ہے کہ تنگدست ہوں میں ، واقف نہیں جو لوگ سفر کے اصول سے سائے کی بھیک مانگ رہے ہیں ببول سے میں آج تک سفر میں ہوں اس اعتماد پر ابھریں گی منزلیں میرے قدموں کی دھول سے

14: ENCOURAGE YOURSELF

"Sometimes when you are in a dark place you think you have been buried but actually you have been planted"

My dear friend, I understand that preparing for competitive exams can feel like an uphill battle, especially when you're facing financial challenges. But remember, your circumstances do not define your potential or your worth.

First and foremost, remind yourself of your strengths and accomplishments. Reflect on how far you've come and the obstacles you've already overcome. Your resilience and determination are your greatest assets, and they will carry you through this journey.

Take pride in your efforts, no matter how small they may seem. Every hour of study, every practice question answered, brings you one step closer to your goals. Celebrate your progress and acknowledge the hard work you're putting in.

Surround yourself with positivity and encouragement. Seek out mentors, teachers, or peers who believe in you and your abilities. Their support and guidance can provide the motivation and reassurance you need to keep going, even when the going gets tough.

Find inspiration in the stories of others who have risen above their circumstances to achieve greatness. Remember that success knows no boundaries – it's not about where you come from, but where you're

headed. Let their journeys inspire you to reach for the stars and pursue your dreams with unwavering determination.

Take care of yourself, both mentally and physically. Practice self-care rituals that nourish your soul and rejuvenate your spirit. Whether it's taking a walk in nature, listening to music, or spending time with loved ones, prioritize activities that bring you joy and peace of mind.

And finally, never lose sight of your dreams. Hold onto them tightly, like precious gems sparkling in the darkness. Let them guide you through the challenges and setbacks, reminding you of the bright future that awaits you on the other side.

You are capable, you are worthy, and you are destined for greatness. Believe in yourself, my friend, and let that belief propel you forward on your journey to success. You've got this!

∧ It's important to remember that we should be just as prepared for failure as we are for success. It's okay to stumble or fall short of our goals, and it's a natural part of the learning process. Let's be kind to ourselves and understand that setbacks are opportunities for growth and improvement.

Success is not guaranteed, and failure is always a possibility. However, it's important not to let failure discourage you from engaging with others and maintaining your self-respect. If you give up and dislike yourself, people may perceive you as weak, which is not beneficial for a student.

خاموش اے دل بھری محفل میں چلانا نہیں اچھا

ادب پہلا قرینہ ہے محبت کے قرینوں میں

15: WHY STRESS

Competitive exams can feel like towering mountains, casting shadows of stress over us. It's not just about answering questions; it's about the weight of expectations, the fear of failure, and the uncertainty of what lies ahead.

Firstly, there's the pressure we put on ourselves. We want to succeed, to prove our worth, and to make ourselves and our loved ones proud. This desire to excel can sometimes transform into a heavy burden, weighing us down with self-doubt and anxiety.

Then, there's the fear of the unknown. The thought of facing questions we might not know the answers to can send shivers down our spine. It's like walking into a dark room, not knowing what's waiting for us on the other side.

Add to that the competition – the feeling of being pitted against countless others, all vying for the same coveted spots. It's easy to feel like a small fish in a vast ocean, swimming against the tide with no guarantee of reaching the shore.

And let's not forget about time pressure. The ticking clock reminds us that every second counts, heightening our sense of urgency and making it hard to catch our breath.

But perhaps what makes competitive exams most stressful is the fear of failure. We worry that if we don't succeed, our dreams will crumble like sandcastles in the tide. The thought of disappointing ourselves and those who believe in us can be paralyzing.

In the end, competitive exams are not just tests of knowledge; they're tests of resilience, perseverance, and mental strength. They push us to our limits, forcing us to confront our fears and overcome obstacles in pursuit of our goals.

So yes, competitive exams are stressful – there's no denying that. But amidst the stress and uncertainty, there's also opportunity – the opportunity to prove ourselves, to grow stronger, and to emerge victorious against all odds. And that, my friend, is what makes the journey worthwhile.

16: OVERCOME STRESS

Preparing for competitive exams can be overwhelming, but it's essential to take care of your mental well-being along the way. Here are some ways to overcome stress during your exam preparation journey:

1. Break it Down: Remember, you don't have to conquer everything all at once. Break your study sessions into smaller, manageable chunks. Focus on one topic or section at a time, and celebrate each small victory along the way.

2. Practice Self-Compassion: Be kind to yourself. Acknowledge that it's okay to feel stressed sometimes. Treat yourself with the same compassion you would offer to a friend facing a similar situation. Remind yourself of your strengths and past achievements.

3. Stay Balanced: While studying is important, don't forget to take breaks and engage in activities that bring you joy and relaxation. Whether it's going for a walk, practicing mindfulness, or spending time with loved ones, make time for activities that recharge your batteries.

4. Healthy Habits: Maintain a healthy lifestyle by prioritizing nutritious meals, regular exercise, and sufficient sleep. A well-nourished body and mind are better equipped to handle stress and retain information effectively.

5. Manage Time Wisely: Create a study schedule that allows for adequate rest and recreation. Set realistic goals and deadlines, and avoid overloading yourself with too much work in a short period. Remember, quality studying is more important than quantity.

6. Seek Support: Don't hesitate to reach out to friends, family, or mentors for support and encouragement. Sharing your concerns and experiences with others can provide valuable perspective and alleviate feelings of isolation.

7. Mindfulness and Relaxation Techniques: Practice mindfulness exercises, deep breathing, or progressive muscle relaxation to calm your mind and body during stressful moments. These techniques can help you stay focused and grounded amidst exam pressure.

8. Visualize Success: Take a moment to visualize yourself succeeding in your exams. Imagine the sense of accomplishment and relief you'll feel when you achieve your goals. Visualizing positive outcomes can boost your confidence and motivation.

9. Stay Positive: Focus on the progress you've made rather than dwelling on setbacks or challenges. Cultivate a positive mindset by reframing negative thoughts into constructive ones. Believe in yourself and your ability to overcome obstacles.

10. Celebrate Milestones: Celebrate your achievements, no matter how small they may seem. Whether it's mastering a difficult concept or completing a practice exam, acknowledge your progress and give yourself credit for your hard work.

Remember, it's normal to feel stressed during exam preparation, but it's essential to take proactive steps to manage it effectively. By prioritizing self-care, staying organized, seeking support, and maintaining a positive mindset, you can navigate through the challenges of exam preparation with resilience and confidence. You've got this!

Vo Jo uthate Hain kirdar per ungaliyan tofe mein unko aaina dijiye

17: BAD GOVERNMENT

A bad government can profoundly impact the future of students in several ways:

1. Education Quality: A government's policies and investments in education directly influence the quality of learning opportunities available to students. A lack of funding, inadequate infrastructure, and outdated curricula can hinder students' ability to receive a quality education, limiting their potential for future success.

2. Access to Education: Poor governance may result in barriers to accessing education, particularly for marginalized groups. This could include issues such as limited school facilities, inadequate transportation, or discriminatory policies that prevent certain students from attending school. Without equal access to education, students' opportunities for advancement are unfairly restricted.

3. Economic Opportunities: Government policies play a significant role in shaping the economy, which in turn affects job prospects and economic opportunities for students after graduation. A mismanaged economy characterized by high unemployment rates, inflation, and limited investment in key sectors can create a bleak outlook for students entering the job market.

4. Political Stability: Instability and unrest caused by bad governance can disrupt the educational environment, leading to school closures, violence, or displacement of students. In such environments, students' ability to focus on their studies and pursue academic goals is severely compromised, jeopardizing their future prospects.

5. Social Services and Support: A government's commitment to social services and support systems, such as healthcare, welfare, and counseling, can significantly impact students' well-being and academic performance. Inadequate social services due to mismanagement or corruption can leave students vulnerable and unable to thrive academically.

6. Research and Innovation: Government investment in research and innovation is crucial for fostering a culture of scientific inquiry and technological advancement. A lack of support for research initiatives and academic institutions can stifle innovation, limiting students' exposure to cutting-edge knowledge and opportunities for intellectual growth.

Overall, a bad government can undermine students' prospects for a bright future by impeding their access to quality education, economic opportunities, social support, and a conducive learning environment. It is essential for governments to prioritize good governance and invest in policies that promote the well-being and success of their future generations.

"In the midst of challenges, remember the strength within you, waiting to be unleashed like a roaring lion. Embrace the journey, for every obstacle is a stepping stone to greatness. Let determination be your compass, guiding you through the darkest of nights. With every setback, let resilience be your armor, shielding you from doubt's cruel arrows. Believe in the power of your dreams, for they are the stars that light your path. And remember, dear student, that the journey may be long, but the destination is worth every trial endured. So rise, shine, and conquer the world with your brilliance."

18: Balancing Studies with Personal Life and Responsibilities

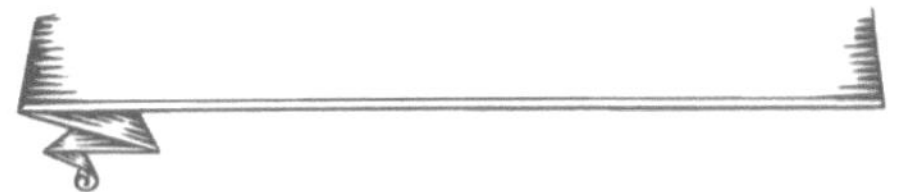

Balancing the demands of academic studies, personal life, and responsibilities while preparing for competitive exams is an emotional journey that delves deep into the human psyche, uncovering layers of resilience, determination, and vulnerability. As I embark on this tumultuous path, I am acutely aware of the weight of expectation that rests upon my shoulders, like Atlas bearing the weight of the world. Each day presents a new set of challenges, a fresh barrage of obstacles to overcome, yet amidst the chaos and uncertainty, there is a flicker of hope that burns bright within my soul.

In the dimly lit confines of my study, I am immersed in a world of textbooks and notes, each page a portal to a realm of knowledge waiting to be explored. The hours stretch into days, the days into weeks, as I pour over equations and theories with a fervor bordering on obsession. But even as I immerse myself in the pursuit of academic excellence, there is a part of me that longs for something more, something beyond the confines of academia. It is in these moments of solitude that I am confronted with the stark reality of my existence, the realization that there is more to life than the pursuit of success.

Yet, even as I grapple with the intricacies of my own emotions, there are responsibilities that demand my attention, obligations that cannot be ignored. The needs of family, the expectations of friends, the duties of everyday life weigh heavily on my mind, pulling me in a thousand different directions at once. And yet, amidst the chaos and clamor of daily life, there is a sense of purpose that guides me, a beacon of light amidst the darkness that surrounds me.

But perhaps the greatest challenge of all lies in finding a balance between my academic pursuits and the intricacies of personal life. The laughter of loved ones, the warmth of companionship, the simple joys of existence beckon to me like distant stars in the night sky, their radiance illuminating the path that lies before me. And yet, even as I reach out to grasp hold of these fleeting moments of happiness, there is a voice in the back of my mind that whispers tales of inadequacy and doubt, casting a shadow over my every endeavor.

It is in these moments of doubt and uncertainty that I am reminded of the fragility of the human spirit, the delicate balance between hope and despair that defines our existence. And yet, even in the darkest of times, there is a glimmer of light that refuses to be extinguished, a flame of resilience that burns bright within my soul. For I am not merely a student preparing for competitive exams; I am a warrior, battling against the forces of doubt and uncertainty with the weapons of knowledge and determination.

But even as I steel myself for the challenges that lie ahead, there are moments of weakness, moments when the weight of expectation threatens to crush my spirit beneath its unyielding weight. The fear of failure, the specter of inadequacy loom large on the horizon, casting a pall of doubt over my every endeavor. And yet, even in the face of adversity, I refuse to surrender to despair, for I know that true strength lies not in the absence of fear, but in the courage to confront it head-on.

It is in these moments of vulnerability that I am reminded of the importance of self-care, of nurturing the body, mind, and soul in equal measure. The simple act of taking a walk in nature, of losing myself in the pages of a favorite book, of spending time with loved ones brings a sense of peace and tranquility that transcends the chaos of daily life. And in these moments of stillness, I find the strength to persevere, to rise above the challenges that threaten to overwhelm me.

But perhaps the greatest lesson I have learned on this journey is the importance of perspective, of viewing the challenges that lie before me not as insurmountable obstacles, but as opportunities for growth and self-discovery. Each setback, each failure is but a stepping stone on the path to greatness, a chance to learn, to evolve, to become the best possible version of myself.

And so, as I continue on this emotional journey of balancing studies with personal life and responsibilities, I do so with a heart full of hope and a spirit unyielding in the face of adversity. For I am not defined by the challenges I face, but by the manner in which I rise above them, emerging stronger and more resilient with each passing day. And though the road ahead may be fraught with obstacles and uncertainties, I walk it with head held high, secure in the knowledge that I am capable of overcoming whatever challenges may come my way.

As the days blend into nights and the nights into days, I find myself grappling with a whirlwind of emotions that threatens to consume me whole. There are moments of triumph, when

I conquer a difficult concept or solve a complex problem, that fill me with a sense of pride and accomplishment. But these moments are fleeting, overshadowed by the ever-present specter of doubt that lurks in the shadows, waiting to pounce at the slightest sign of weakness.

It is in these moments of doubt and uncertainty that I am reminded of the sacrifices that I have made along the way. The countless hours spent poring over textbooks instead of spending time with loved ones, the missed opportunities for adventure and exploration, the dreams deferred in the pursuit of academic excellence. And yet, even as I grapple with the weight of these sacrifices, there is a part of me that knows they were not made in vain.

For every sacrifice made is a testament to my unwavering dedication and commitment to my goals. It is a reminder that success is not given but earned through hard work, perseverance, and sacrifice. And though the road may be long and fraught with challenges, I take solace in the knowledge that every step brings me closer to realizing my dreams.

But even as I strive to strike a balance between my academic pursuits and personal life, there are moments when the scales tip precariously out of balance. The demands of exams and deadlines often take precedence over the needs of family and friends, leaving me feeling torn between duty and desire. It is a delicate dance, a balancing act that requires finesse and skill, yet one that I am determined to master.

And so, I soldier on, drawing strength from the love and support of those who stand by my side, cheering me on in moments of triumph and lifting me up in moments of despair. Their unwavering belief in my abilities fuels the fire that burns within my soul, propelling me ever forward on this emotional journey of self-discovery and growth.

But perhaps the greatest challenge of all lies in finding the courage to confront my own fears and insecurities, to silence the voices of doubt that threaten to hold me back. It is a battle that rages within me, a constant struggle to believe in myself when the world seems to conspire against me. And yet, even in the darkest of times, there is a glimmer of hope that refuses to be extinguished, a belief in my own potential that burns bright within my heart.

And so, I press on, my heart heavy with the weight of expectation yet buoyed by the promise of a brighter tomorrow. For I know that every obstacle I overcome, every challenge I face, brings me one step closer to realizing my dreams. And though the journey may be fraught with hardship and adversity, I walk it with head held high, secure in the knowledge that I am not alone. For I am surrounded by the love and support of those who believe in me, who see in me a strength and resilience that I sometimes struggle to see in myself.

And so, as I continue on this emotional journey of balancing studies with personal life and responsibilities, I do so with a sense of purpose and determination that burns brighter than ever before. For I know that the challenges I face today will only serve to make me stronger tomorrow. And though the road ahead may be long and fraught with obstacles, I walk it with a heart full of hope and a spirit unyielding in the face of adversity. For I am not merely a student preparing for competitive exams; I am a warrior, fighting for my dreams with every ounce of strength and determination that I possess. And though the journey may be difficult, I know that the destination will be more than worth the struggle.

19: SUCCESS STORIES

> **Dr. Abdus Salam:** A Pakistani theoretical physicist, Dr. Abdus Salam became the first Muslim Nobel laureate in science when he won the Nobel Prize in Physics in 1979 for his contribution to electroweak unification. Despite facing discrimination due to his religious background, Dr. Salam's dedication to his field and groundbreaking research serves as a beacon of inspiration for students pursuing careers in science and academia.

> **Malala Yousafzai:** Malala Yousafzai, a Pakistani education activist, survived a targeted assassination attempt by the Taliban at a young

age for advocating girls' education. Undeterred by the threat to her life, Malala continued to speak out and became the youngest-ever Nobel Prize laureate at the age of 17. Her courage, resilience, and commitment to education inspire students to stand up for their beliefs and pursue their goals despite adversity.

> **Mo Farah:** Born in Somalia, Mo Farah overcame numerous challenges, including fleeing war-torn Somalia as a child refugee and adapting to a new life in the UK. Despite facing obstacles, Farah pursued his passion for running and became one of the most decorated long-distance runners in history, winning multiple Olympic and World Championship titles. His story teaches students the importance of perseverance, hard work, and resilience in achieving their dreams.

> **Ibn Khaldun:** A renowned Muslim scholar, Ibn Khaldun made significant contributions to various fields, including sociology, historiography, and economics, during the 14th century. His seminal work, "The Muqaddimah," laid the foundation for modern social sciences and is still studied today. Ibn Khaldun's intellectual curiosity, critical thinking, and dedication to scholarship serve as an inspiration for students pursuing academic excellence and intellectual inquiry.

> **Sultan Qaboos bin Said Al Said:** Sultan Qaboos, the former Sultan of Oman, transformed his country from a poor, isolated nation into a prosperous and modern state during his reign. Despite facing internal and external challenges, Sultan Qaboos's visionary leadership, strategic vision, and commitment to

development paved the way for Oman's progress and prosperity. His story inspires students to aspire to leadership roles and make a positive impact on their communities and societies.

> **<u>Abraham Lincoln:</u>** Despite numerous failures and setbacks throughout his life, including multiple lost elections and business ventures, Abraham Lincoln persevered and eventually became one of the most influential leaders in American history. His story exemplifies the power of resilience, determination, and never giving up on one's dreams.

> **<u>Sundar Pichai:</u>** From humble beginnings in India to becoming the CEO of Google and Alphabet Inc., Sundar Pichai's journey is a testament to the transformative power of education and hard work. His story inspires

students to dream big, set ambitious goals, and relentlessly pursue them.

> **Mary Kom:** Overcoming financial hardships and societal barriers, Mary Kom emerged as one of the world's most successful boxers, winning numerous championships and Olympic medals. Her journey from a small village in Manipur to global sporting prominence inspires students to overcome obstacles and pursue their passions with dedication and perseverance.

Mastering Competitive Exams

About the Author

Hello! My pen name is K.Ahram and I am a beginner writer. Writing has been a passion of mine for as long as I can remember, but I have only recently mustered the courage to share my work with others. As a beginner, I understand that I have much to learn about the craft and I am excited to explore new genres, styles, and techniques. I am eager to connect with other writers, receive feedback on my work, and continue to improve my skills. Though I am just starting out on this writing journey, I am determined to learn and grow as a writer and share my stories with the world.

Writing is a way to explore the depths of my imagination, express my thoughts and emotions, and connect with others through the power of storytelling, I find immense joy in the process of putting pen to paper or fingers to keyboard.